LATE BREAKING
A.E. Stringer

salmonpoetry

Published in 2013 by
Salmon Poetry
Cliffs of Moher, County Clare, Ireland
Website: www.salmonpoetry.com
Email: info@salmonpoetry.com

Copyright © A.E. Stringer, 2013

ISBN 978-1-908836-48-9

COVER DESIGN: *Mary McDonnell*
COVER ART: *Nelleke Beltjens*
TYPESETTING: *Siobhán Hutson*

Printed in Ireland by Sprint Print

to the memory of my mother,

Marianne Hobert Stringer

(1925-2009)

Acknowledgements

In earlier versions some of the poems in this book appeared in these journals and collections:

ABZ: "Lightest Night of the Year" "My Father Asleep"
Artful Dodge: "Half-Lives"
Colorado Review: "The Architecture of Sunlight"
Confluence: "End of August"
First Circle: "Lichening"
The Journal: "Intermedial" (formerly "Half-Life Matters")
Kansas Quarterly: "Sinkholes"
Kestrel: "Turtle Crossing" "Visual Manifest"
Mississippi Valley Review: "The Stairs, From Above"
Poetry Sky (online): "Interlude"
Prairie Schooner: "The Evolution Of Rock 'n Roll" "Kings of Boogie"
Riverwind: "River Dance"
Tygerburning Literary Journal: "Artificial Horizon" "Rapture Monday" "When in Rome" "Hank's Wall Street Tavern and Piano Bar"

"My Friend Told Me" was first published in *Backcountry: Contemporary Writing in West Virginia* edited by Irene McKinney (Morgantown, Vandalia Press, 2002). Copyright by the West Virginia University Press.

Additional acknowledgement to Marshall University, the Virginia Center for the Creative Arts, and the Mid-Atlantic Arts Foundation for their support of my work.

Once more, deepest thanks to family, friends, and colleagues for their help and inspiration.

Special thanks to Duane and Joyce Taylor on Crystal Glen Farm, to Mitch and Don in the Northeast, to Mike and Doc in Cleveland, and to Mary, one more time.

The supernatural is only the natural disclosed.

EMILY DICKINSON

And somewhere in the upper story the Architect
uncertain whether to dance or genuflect.

PAULA MEEHAN

Contents

$\tilde{1}$

Landscape with Waterfall

after Hiroshige

Style of a hanging screen
scaled down, monochromatic,
museum print no wider
than my hand. High country
runoff threads through
sheer rock, snowmelt falling
as rain, foreground
hint of plum blossom.
Two roofs—wood smoke?

Here south of February,
a skim of snow glazes a stream
near thaw. Step into the scene

full scale: late leaves
fallen. By inexplicable craft,
they have come to be
embedded to the depth
of hand prints. The ice
traces each outline, ever
faithful. Underneath, a sheet
of water flowing—soundless—
over shelves of bedrock.

Artificial Horizon

Someone invented it
to correct disorientation.
To make his approach, a pilot
matches the tangent of land's end
to the pitch of his plane.
Foggy weather, he reads
the line on the dial.

The actual device just
a fancy spirit level, you may
posit more romantic origins
for the name. Consider mist
thickening offshore as water
and sky fuse. Though never
really there, horizon dissolves.

Standing on the point, you know
beyond the gray that line remains.
You call it by name, say you see it
even though the eye cannot.
Ergo, believer, such imaginary
lines divide the physical
from the metaphysical.

Plato would laud your system's
fine distinctions, who claimed
ideals inhere beyond the flat
world's edge, that a word
draws airy absence down
to level ground incarnate.
Therein lies the artifice.

Glider Flight

One with wind he floats
inside unearthly silence.
Like the canopy bubble,
his head is a drop of pure
pressure as updrafts answer
his prayer for a longer
ride. A gull pitches up
the one o'clock distance.
Loops of tumult clip
spoils from the wings.
Peaks appear closer, rustle
of pine, then a nosedive
tilts his rolling eyes
toward home. Horizon
and its muffled cloud-line
rise, wheeling, center
the glider on a random
landmark. Low whine
and windmill spiral.
Head sleepy with g-force
and torque in a dizzy
kiss of air, he hears
the rocks talk him down.

Mineral Ambition

If sand can aspire to be castle
or marine clay the perfect vessel,
then a rock may imagine locomotion.
The ore within assays its former
stardom, burning for a beholding
eye, as the rock now dreams itself
atop the shoulders of a dancer

gliding tangential. Mindful
of return to the metamorphic,
it marvels how suddenly desire
fulfilled renames itself grace
and is replaced. Already gaining
weight, the rock feels grainier as
pirouettes and spins diminish

earthbound, breathtaken. Why
oceans don't spill. Mindless
again, it lies inert in breaker foam
but sea–changed, a rock once
aware, once awhirl, a rock
a precious stone at last on which
a human foot steps in time.

Allegheny Highland

If the man in the moon wore a hat,
he might tip it, smiling diplomat
immune to human law. Look long
and earthly boulders glare back, oddly
channeled brows and stark, embodied
poses no longer inanimate.

East of tonight, tomorrow breaks
over slopes re-grooved by wind and rain.
Under the grins of fractal monuments,
the land rocks in muddy intercourse.

Held to the ear by hand, a stone
will verify its unlikely sentience,
whispering of pressure-cracks
and ancient, molten evenings.

Death Valley from Zabriskie Point, 1942

after the photograph by Ansel Adams

Great bed unmade, quilt shifted
over bodies unseen. Wizening
ranges, the landscape gathers
northward in parallel folds.
Rampant waffling deepens
the field and burns in a dream
of blessed dusk. Seventy years.

Gray in the photo, likely violet
shadows overflowed the sand
and moon-swept rocks, combed
riverruns so dry the fanned-out
valleys trembled. Tableau
of absence, sleepless wind stirring
the bottom of an ancient sea.

Dolphin Sign

Mist just visible on my glasses,
improbably tiny beads convened.
A dolphin—is it?—dips and pivots
in the canal behind my sister's house.

Low tide, they seldom swim this far
into the maze of channels and docks.
A few concentric ripples, then
the curved dorsal fin appears, rides

the arc of the body back below. Even
at fifty yards, it makes for an event.
Naturally we want more. Distant
gong. Scanning for new ripples

in a surface that mirrors the gray
undersea of sky, we wait for another
breach, quick spray from a blowhole
to let us know how much we know

is mist, how much just breathing.

Genetic Non-Pigmentation in Deer, Interpreted

They want to live among us, deer do,
delicious suburban lawns and broad
green shrubbery a few leaping strides
from the wooded verge. They pick their
way through open ground at dusk,
shadowing their young in ever-larger
numbers, only to spook at motion-sensor
lights, slammed doors, human whispers.
Their sepia bodies look too much
like our ancestors'. Turning white tails,
they bound back to aging poplars
and spotted salamanders, to the princess
pine beside the hummingbird caught
dead in the Velcro of burdock, each

thing delicate, hungry, hunted. But
one of them must not be killed, despite
Mr. Darwin's rule of natural selection.
For it is said the rare albino deer grazes
these fields in predawn as if standing under
perpetual snowfall. In telescopic sights
her pink eyes shine, impossible to fathom.
What stops the trigger finger is not the law,
not astonishment, not enchantment,
but pure superstition. And if anything
deserves divine payback, surely killing
a creature from a fairytale qualifies. For
the price of its meat is car wrecks, cancer
to loved ones, financial ruin, trees fallen

on houses, the hunter a marked man,
a convert, from the moment he chooses
wrong. Your tail white as all the rest,
do you wonder at their earthen coats
and dark noses? You, white as the moon,
white as the heat of a star so rare
only radio waves betray it, so far off
it will not melt a single snowflake, white
as the noise of traffic bearing down, white
as low sun hazing the marsh pond, filling
your glassy red and blinking eyes, white
as a newborn in a leafy grove in spring,
white as its teeth and hooves, so bright
that we must be your only shadows.

Coyote

for Duane and Joyce

Shuffle of shadow in earshot,
barely: still, at a hundred yards
commotion enough and cause

for alert. Gray form hustling
in winter woods, too gangly for a fat
raccoon or young bear, you made

no sense, gone in seconds,
the three of us left rustling daylight
in fallen leaves, too mystified

to keep quiet. Track and scat
had led us there, within a shout
of your vanishing. How can I

not know what I've seen? All
the time, so here's your name to give
this story heft. Yet you remain

a blur, a wager I'm no good for,
these lines more about those
other mates, *failure* and *desire*.

Deep In a Jackal's Dream

Thin as a desert sundial
you shadowed the dead gazelle.
Nightfall now, crest of a dune,

you commence to writhing
among specters of kills
devoured on the sly. Blood

of your boiling blood, you wolfed
spoiled flesh with bits of hide.
Be glad their touchy souls

bare only ghostly teeth.
Drowse on, quiver in cool sand
as another nightmare wracks

hindquarters, then the heart:
half cry, half bark, and nerves
studded with struggle,

for what you do not pursue
in daylight, you are doomed
to scavenge at night.

Birdwatch Practicum

for John Van Kirk

How slight the finch, yet more so
when we scan toward the call
maybe forty yards away, perch
obscured in a maple down the slope.
Quick study, a bird in binoculars.
With fields of view small as a grape-
fruit at arm's length, don't try to

follow it through the green to
catch the moment's flutter. The new
breeds limb to limb as we learn
to focus on any fleeting detail,
never inconsequential: telltale
of tree form, neck blaze, or sweet
song. All is bird, or not, if we seek

what means only to elude us.
Stepping lightly toward the quick,
we cultivate the art of seeing anything
of moment, that is, everything
except the alleged tanager. So rare
in summer, such red is certain
to stand out, tantalize, disappear.

Why Mullet Breach

Some guess perpetual itch
even a so-called fish has to scratch
on the fly, lacking other means,
fins instead of wings.

Maybe a dip upward
in air tips the scales, cheers
the livelier citizens of the bay.
No one really knows.

Anyhow mullet, like birds,
have gizzards, aspire perhaps
to a leafy feast hovering
higher than it seems, above

the ceiling of the water.
In a classic case a Florida man
locked up for fishing on Sunday
proved mullet are not fish

legally. They do not eat
their own. So he walked, free to fish
again, to dream of loopholes
and leaping through.

Turtle Crossing

Running near oblivious
I feel the first tickle
of Achilles tendon heat.
Off right, a rusty shuffle.
I can't resist I stop
on the shoulder where low
growth rustles. The source
trundles toward me
like clumsy wind
parting Florida scrub.

The shell has evolved
to keep this plodding
from harm. A pause,
and instinct draws her in.
Genuflect, and my heel
sears. *What do you say?*
She's well beyond such
condescending small talk
anyhow. Yet by the jut
or dip of her head, she
measures my slightest move.
She does not aim to yield.

Perhaps a race
with a fleeter man calls
for she skirts me and
clears the road in what
seems like nothing flat.
I rise to watch her

wobble off, a helmet
riding amphibious feet.

In Zeno's paradox
Achilles can't believe
that slow-and-steady will
at last outpace him.
The crux of the nonsense
is the unreal distance
shrinking to all
but zero between them.

No hurry now, I trot off
softly as moss, no will
to jostle the earth still
balanced on her shell,
and miles to go. No, ages.

Great Bear Dancing on a Ball

Piqued by catcalls, dying
whoops and sighs in the icy glare,
she ducked into a cave too small
and slept off the north star.
Some solstice. It would
have foiled a minor bear.
Her gut, resonant as a dream
of bees, rumbled. A few moons
flared past the opening.
When floes ran blue she rose
to birdsong blinking, lumbered
looney over muddy fields
wearing a gauzy dress. It fit her
just so. On it like smears,
imagine dogwoods with
real blossoms butterflied.

Dominion

Inside its riddled bark, the dogwood's
truncated mind thinks—if you can call
a tree's lucidity after what humans fail
so miserably to do—it *thinks* I'm a mild
miracle for wrestling sidetracked branches
free of the loops and hooks of grapevine.
Plus, the prolific honeysuckle has run

a petaled staircase up and over its crown,
dragging half the tree down in a wave.
Even the slow-witted crepe myrtle long ago
reckoned sideways was the only way
to outreach these creepers for sunlight.
With little spirit and less reason, I'm down
here sweating and bleeding for a tree

a couple of winters from dead. Just
hacking and jerking for my health, dust
sifting through shade beneath the hopeless
tangle. Tomorrow's cardinals may sense
it makes a difference, their green cover
blown. The old dogwood gives up a few
dead limbs—willingly, I'd like to think.

Prevailing Dust

swirls eastward from the windswept Gobi,
its barren interior overgrazed and ever-
wider with lost trees and deserted wells.
It falls from brown skies over Beijing, a few
thousand tons a month choking the cyclists.
It surges across the Pacific on tides of ozone
and pollen, arsenic and chaff and ash,

a dust storm over water absurd as pigs
in flight. Odd how the fish keep hatching
healthy as rats, and empty islands bloom
incredibly on nutrients from nowhere.
Tropic rain cannot dampen it. No other
word for it? Take mine. Tainted plumes
infuse the clouds all the way to California,

a glut perpetually arriving. Bound east
across time zones, it coats leaf and book,
every last parked car, and bends the dusk
into phenomenal sunset images, shades
of *orange* and rhymes unheard-of. Split
second, I uncap my lens for a long shot
so breathtaking it's lethal to behold.

My Friend Told Me

for Eric Nelson

When he came upon the family cat
convulsing, chin bubbled with drool,
he recognized the signs of another
poisoned cat, great dry heaves

vivid since childhood. The strain
of mercy: he wrangled the hopeless form
into a pillowcase, then into a sinkful
of water and held on until the writhing

stilled. He buried it. He washed his hands.
When his children pretty soon asked
after the lost cat, he told them—love's
gray lie—he had found it already gone.

And here is the grave, he showed them,
as his own father had done, truth told
slant. Father to no one, I listen closely,
put my life in his children's hands.

Lichening

Beside a rushing stream, my friend
says lichen is the most primitive
of plants, kissed in the first symbiosis.
After blue-green algae arose,
fungi broke up the rocks for food.
Water and air, the fiery biosphere,
bedecked the earth in good time.

Even now, the elements move
the living. We collar our coats in wind,
shrug them for the sun. Mist thickens,
rises, rains to swell another stream
we might yet pass beside, lichening,
airing similar matters. Old friend,
the rocks shall have our bodies then.

Still and All

Down to roots unmoved, the trees
barely list across the flat blue
morning sky following the first
sure freeze of November
when low sun—not wind, not just
chill—coaxes a shower of leaves
from the mesh of limbs above.

Staring up from the ground floor
I guess Galileo could explain. Not
about Jupiter's moons, which he called
by name, but how all bodies fall
from leaning towers equally. Still,
the shrivel of each leaf fixes the track
and rate of its descent. Further,

a sheen of thawed frost surely
alters drag. A shapely maple flutters,
tumbles through random radiance,
red. A sleeker beech glides down
a spiral staircase, aerodynamic.
A few, tight as fists, wobble
as gravity lowers them, reeling

out fine lines from celestial spools.
Tensed as a tree, I am entranced
by all falling, a moveable stillness:
hundreds in the air at once
ticking branches. A hum climbs
my legs, through back and neck
arches. Murmur and sway, as if

death might as well dawn anytime.
Finally a gust in the upper reaches
frees another myriad. Glad my fancy
goes ungranted, I straighten up
light-headed and look down:
how the earth floats far below,
the ground's mosaic transformed.

In a pool at my feet, reflections
of the fall articulate skyward. Melting
through its orbit, the cobalt moon,
not far from impact, cues my eyes
horizonward. In a field beyond
the trees, the sun sparks ten thousand
moons in the drop-stippled grass.

~ ~

2

You, Untitled

for Mary McDonnell

Sketchy at first, traipsing earth: tall, blond,
and fair, you were bound for the elements,
head tilting skyward for birdsong.
Then I saw the paintings.

In the studio, a wood panel preoccupied
the floor, sprawled. Down thick edges the drip
trails recalled every color you'd tried—
mixed and thinned and brushed
and combed across the surface with
whatever sprig the forest had given you.
Call it *painting*, lacking another word—
as much trapdoor as window.
I could not stand too close.

Blackberry Winter: blue tint hesitant then radiant yellow a model a
perpendicularity, the flaws as always desires, trails in territories heretofore.

Expressionist. Abstract. As if a word
matters as much as how to see. At our feet,
the visual may be a surface to cross
or pass through, and the hands *made*
for crafting two dimensions, by which
we gather *depth is defined* (and god
comes down to earth). A word may
be a gesture but *tone is everything*,
you said, tone of the field and of the fields
beneath it, through layers of paint
into the raw wood. Hung across my path

like a web, that's a painting: synopsis
of form and line of sight, absolutely
nothing of moment left out.

Still Point: yellow aglow through the red, dawnscape wavering, hint of
blue shadow, iris of some eye unclouded.

Swept across the wood, the grit in the paint finds its place.
Liquid thinner refines it while a barberry whisk scores the mix
across grain and layer, wavering grid of horizons and
perpendiculars: the frame's way of entering the art. You step
around it, leaning in, whole body given to this map of instances.
The work holds the floor always, so nothing falls off, falls far.

Weeks later you stand the piece up and walk away as far as
walls allow, look long and level at its diminished rectangle.
Now a new magic passes between, impressions reified.
Random imperfections of unremembered movement make
natural focal points, like flecks on a leaf. How to read them:
only at a distance. Then find a rise in a field that first looked
flat, a place to see beyond from.

After: the blue and the black, right side in wash and veil, flow and delta
of darker value, and to the left a depth of red, green, magenta emergent.

As cardinal directions fix the compass rose,
so this crosshatch weathers the texture
of the painting becoming perpetual, a world
without human figures: ground and plain,
line and interstice, all process
in a stillness that can't be still. Something
of you dissolved in the act of making

the way colors blend in thinning spirits.
Abstract might only mean
follow along. Until the unseeable is.

Late Blue: harsh lines fade, edges blurred to rainswept seas, artificial horizon, color itself a language of signs.

All your *Untitleds* propped against the wall, one behind the other, like memories attending the present and bleeding through it. *Expressionist* might only mean *the listener who listens.* Hang a whole show, twenty different doors, one house.

Every word, I see now, comes to silence
although the right one (here the prayer
goes) may somehow stir a loss
to feel as if it's healing, and titles merely scars.
These might say what I see or saw or thought
and not what you painted, surely not.

For all I know you will roam ceaselessly,
bent to the next work as if wading,
reaching your hands into it like some
long-legged shorebird dragging
the earth at bottom. A stricken wildness
will rise through the floor, as *duende*
through the soles of a dancer.
Suddenly wings. Standing
the painting up, laying it back down,
touching up over and over, you coax
the visual into a fabric so sheer
egrets fly through like summer snow.

~~~

3

River Dance

Standing quick at a strike, great
grandfather's blood pools in his feet.
Hook slipped, the pole whips,
        implies he cannot
find his center, so rocks the boat
        in time to faint,
slant music. Not even clouds
float so loftily so long. Rainfall.

In spring, birds or wind rose
bearing seed. Such consummate
efforts also could not
        soar forever.
All ten thousand things fall
actually. The lightest leaf
        shudders
earthward like an man off–
balance, arms now doodling air.
        Newborn
drawn from mother's weightless
middle, he pitches into the flow.

Earth wants him back
is all. A lucky fish glides off
as easily as river runs down great
        grandfather's inner ear. There
in semi-circular canals the current
stills, as he does, castaway
        on any plausible island.

God of Nightmares

Dreadful scenario nearly
a howl, and I resurface,
dim bedroom walls crawling.
Adaze, I lose the harrowing
thread, assume as usual
another narrow escape.
Deal me out Morpheus, you

and your eyefuls of sand.
I'm fishing the silence. Damn
all that dazzle of tricks you sweep
over my sails: vicious dogs,
dizzy falls, knives, floods.
You know our hearts can flag
on the black high seas of sleep,

stray so far we're lost in sheets,
adventure turned to elegy.
For the crying daylights,
I remember that hurricane,
a deaf child wild with terror.
She kept watching my hands
for signs of survivors.

Sinkholes

As groundwater levels fall, Florida
caves under the weight, literally
malled into the ground. Structures, cars,
a thousand squatters every day.
No one can stop them settling here.
It's warm, and the fat snowbirds.

Gravelly layers below won't hold up.
Even automated sprinklers undermine
the unsettling. As if land mines planted
long ago were triggered, random
craters swallow the unsuspecting.

An earthquake or a hundred-year flood
will undo a region, victims joined
in misery's one lifeboat. But a sinkhole
is personal, chasm opened at my feet
while Bridget next door hangs her sheets,
mouth a more perfect zero than my yard.

For thirty million years Florida could breathe
underwater. Now the seas must rise
to flush the land's wounds with salt
and oil. Then the trees will bare
their limbs above the glutted markets.

Channel Remote

Captives of the Florida summer,
I watch him watch TV all afternoon.
Recall dimmed, neural network gummed
with plaque the docs can't peel back to pink,
my father's on the road to disengagement,
riding shotgun in his easy chair. Forget
the years and genetics, all those channels
could fluster any genius: reality spinoffs,
classic reruns, endless talk.

Out of character, he surfs the obscure
shallows of Suncoast Cable until he
finds what he can follow, settling on
Ultimate Fighting bouts or on the World's
Most Amazing Videos: cop chases, ultralights
in downdrafts, hydrofoils gone airborne,
and loopy daredevils leaping four-wheelers
without irony over vintage steamboats,
not quite making it. Better than

losing your keys for the third time today.
These stories are short—gravity a nimbler
antagonist than time—the plots all climax—
broken ribs or burns in the first degree
rated "Mature." Unlike careening markets,
disaster reports, or American foreign policy,
this news is often good: a lucky man walks away
from the wreckage, ahead of him a longer
and wiser life than he will ever remember.

My Father Asleep

As evening broke, family chatter over,
my father retired to the news, his body
spreading on the couch like milk
spilled into a saucer. He drifted off,
he had to, wrung out by telephones,
boned of the day's unnatural shocks.
We lived it up all through his house.

Now understand, while the clock circled
the office tower, he worked the years
into shadows that I might lie down
tonight in his age, exhausted in my own
living room, bathed in the glow
of prime-time shows ever implausible.
I can't keep his eyes open.

Visual Manifest

1

If, as lore has it, a newborn's cry
could clear a blind man's eyes, how then
would the birth room appear? Glistening
mother and child breathing, the midwife
wringing out her cloths, the father
with fewer words for this than for
a wall of pure white. He is not blind.

2

Six days a week, Sister keeps
her eyes downcast, a sign of humility
to the everywhere God of her Order.
On the seventh day, vow of silence
continuing, she is permitted
to look up, to feast after a long fast.
The phenomenal world is delicious.

3

Equally blessed is the awe that follows
a long-denied first sight, breath-
less *oh!* Hungry seekers working
a forest glade at first see none,
then mushroom after mushroom
appears for the plucking, as when
fine-tuning turns to music.

4

Likewise a lost hiker may not notice
vultures cruising overhead. There.
Then he spots another, another until
the sky swells and, pointing variously,
he thinks they have come from inside
his eye, as medieval artists believed
the very light of day did.

5

An ancient theater's two-storey curtains
hang heavy as wet blankets. Threadbare
velvet shines almost metallic. But stare
long enough, just before the film, and
see them sway in subtle updrafts
of shadow. Now previews, titles,
then scene one: sunrise, lullaby.

Washing Mother's Hair

The last time you were healing,
Florida's drought deepened.
"Feel better if it would rain,"
you said, pain of hard ground
and grass browning. Stems of the rain
lilies drooped, blooms delayed.
You step, halting, into the shower,
settle in a rusted patio chair.
The water soothes to the bone.
Of time you take a measure,
though it's gravity that never
relents. Even at eighty-six pounds,
arising is one more chore you must do
for me. Lathering the baby shampoo
I remember you younger,
swimming us to the deep end
of the big pool. We stayed
afloat on your voice. Gray
strands clinging to your ears, eyes
closed and up-tilted, you ease
under the spray to rinse, the question
mark of your spine still
standing for answer. On this
we all depend. The monsoon
showers have come this June—
you said they would—rain lilies
unbowed, pink and delicate
as they are, as little time
as they have.

Intensive Care

for Jeff Jeske

Among the knotted lifelines your face
is not your own, swollen from the sepsis
and the cures, as if *Invasion of the Body
Snatchers* had bred a new, unearthly you.
Such a mask alarms, passing strange.
Old friend, today I am your brother,
magic word at the ICU checkpoint.
In photos on the mirror, you're younger,
decked out at one of Doc's weddings or
beaming at your girls. We've all grown newer,
gloomier faces since. Organ rhythms tied
to meds and ventilator, you're away but
can't be gone, chart-tracks like runes,
grainy as mountains on the moon.

One eye glued shut, one an icy squint,
you stay afloat on a sea of science and
streptococcus A. Deep in foundering lungs,
lives too small to be seen are blinking out
by the thousands. Back to hell, praise be,
and damn the password. The monitors
are terse as sentinels, vital *blip* and *hum*
counterpointing your return. Inside this
three-week vigil, maybe you can hear us:
crosstalk of stories cut with *amens* and sighs
like some alien mosaic or a scene from *Cries
and Whispers.* What you won't remember
of that other world, we can't forget in this.
How the old days seem so holy now.

"Surrender Dorothy"

Clever ambiguities aside, it's not
some god but the Wicked Witch
who smokes up the sky with warning,
more fearsome than a twister any day
with her winged monkeys, baritone
guards, and bad spells. I mean, that
broom could set your face on fire.

Yet once you've been through Oz,
the polished lanes and emerald towers,
poppies' brilliance lingering, no
screeching hag in a cloud will get you,
my pretty, nor your little dog. Spun
dreaming from the vortex onto golden
bricks, you and your motley retinue

step to the anthem of wonderland.
What a band: classic rationalist
stuffed with shocks of straw men;
tin man waxing romantic, the echo
of his rusted drum; and the King—
not Prince—of the Forest a-swagger
until a telling tail rattles him.

Dorothy, with friends like these, be
glad the witch and water don't mix,
and the wizard, too human by miles,
floats off, *ex machina*, on his own
hot air. Be glad for Toto, too, his nose
tracing the gist behind the reverie:
you have yourself, the ruby slippers.

Star Party

The dress code called for black, and
a marquee name was pledged. Beamers
and Infiniti's grazed on a classy ranch
in the Hamptons. The little people
would feel the larger, forking out thousands
for the worthy cause of equine rescue.
Inside the mansion, a star from the West
winked, million-dollar smile, elbows
polished iridescent on the inner circle.

Hung with earpieces and gold chains,
security goons adorned all doors.
The darklings milled outside the ropes,
so far from the festive bonfire they
could not see each other, let alone
the black benches they kept upsetting
(bruises appeared in the morning).
They seethed to meet the heroine of screen
and gossip column, who did not wish

to be a star so wished-upon
by such a mob. Glenlivet enlivened
their anonymity. At last the star was borne
to the veranda to greet her fitful subjects.
She knew they must be out there
agog, though mere and far, rumors
of dark matter. How vast the universe,
she thought, ice in tumblers glinting,
how curious these terrestrials.

Hank's Wall Street Tavern and Piano Bar

A friendly quip. Everyone gets it, walking in.
It's not Wall Street, thank bloody heaven, and there's
no piano anymore. We'd be sitting on it, or under.
Pure hyperbole. Damn if this ain't still the grandest
hole-in-the-wall it's ever been my pleasure to drink
myself groggy in. Beth Ann took on the place, kept
the name, Mary the barkeep extraordinaire, Ed
the union-man-Shakespearian, and Joe the fixer
of shiny wrecks just a few of the friends I find here—
not rain nor sleet nor snow shall keep us—crackpot
armchair skeptics all, fine folk what made a stand
in the mountain state of hardluck West Virginia, my
home-sweet-not-too-far-away-from-home, where years
of curveball-midlife-getting-by got my name put down too,

in the trusty book of citizens naturalized by booze.
Here our lives converge, among the faded halos left
by icy bottles, beyond the lies that put this rail-and-
river town on the map. Don't think the fish tank's
just another metaphor, or red leather booths the seat
of passion. Just dig the classic tunes, the dart lane,
and a bar that runs as far as you can follow,
back to the wall if you dare to spill what ails you
and take on characters as bold as one more Maker's
on the rocks. For here the downbeat mind expands,
no irony, in the smallest pub in the heart of the city.
Last call, it's the walls that keep us close, mirrors
doubling our chances, until some old man raving
Rapture! nods off at last, and we take his keys.

When in Rome

Glass–clatter backstatic, I wonder aloud
Who got the flowers? At the bar, no one
seems to fathom. All of us lately numbed
by travesty, atrocity, bull, the sudden
gift of such a rosy outlook cheers.
Still the next Nero draws his bow.

There's no choice the stoic bartender
allows. News-bites crawl the screen,
lurid footage, refugees, tainted oceans.
Into what pretzel folly is our dough
twisted and baked. *Nation of dolls*
the cool dresser says to his date. *Play
house* the girl seems to reply, odd spell
broken by a call from the grill: *order up!*

Virtual Baby

In the arms of anyone's daughter,
a big-eyed, baby-faced effigy rocks
fussy to a fault: rubber, rayon, foam
and pressure-molded, who knows
how she moves? *It's alive* the voiceover
wails, thrilled as the mad doctor
at the stirring of his concocted friend.

Likely a spring hinge for a shoulder,
a plastic bottle bonded to her teensy hand,
the nipple finds her mouth each time
she seems to help herself—imagine
sweet milk passing between them.
Batteries included, and a crying shame.
Little girls will raise these little girls

until none of them ever grows up.
No living doll, this baby's blues
never close. Aglaze, they are fixed
on miracle mom, a human child
who one day learns she too may birth
a moving likeness, with no more love
than what it takes to raise the dead.

One Hundred and Seventy Million Dead

by estimates, the total casualties of war, torture, terror, and political,
ethnic, and sectarian violence in the last century

The Aboriginals roamed the wrong lands.
The Jew bled the wrong blood.
The Russian spun the wrong story.
The Tutsi worshipped the wrong god.
The Chinese marched in the wrong square.
The American worked in the wrong tower.
Thy will be undone: last week eight Bosnians
fell full of arrows. So the century has taught us
only this: how much imagination it takes
to keep the killing lively.

If the instruments of torture could recount
their stories like the nightly news, if we
could stand over their dark contours
demanding answers as the great butchers
did, through howls of innocence, then
might we admit a fresh, superior hell
had finally been wrought on earth.

If history is theater and posterity
a captive audience, the actors holding
stained blades to our throats might be
our ancestors: a run for all the ages.
Imagine such a company setting and striking
each of one hundred and seventy million
tragedies, playing the innocent dead
in accord with Stanislavsky's method,
without surprise.

The Alternatives

My wife, bless her heart, was beset
by demons. I was not one, if on-and-off
so it seemed. Her superior, an inferior
character, had unjustly assailed her again,
as the mean will vilify their paragons.
Three weeks tracing the edge of her wits
and I've come close enough
to see how far those depths go down.
I was just thinking of the philandering soul

whose girlfriend splashed his face with a brew
of Coke and lye. No one could look at him
though once, in passing, she glanced
at her work, and it was good. Reveries
of revenge might sustain us in extremes,
but please, dears, let us mull no actual
evil. Reading of cretin vandals, my wife
swears she would work cheaply,
if the local cemetery ever hired security.
I was just thinking of the undertaker

who flew to a strange city to embalm
his father. What dignity remained the son
could barely guess. He only knew
the heart was overdue, that the older man
had slipped away making love
to the woman he loved. I can see my wife,
cell phone, sealed beam, and pepper spray,
driving elliptical lanes among memorials
protecting the dead from the living.

Freak Experience

The cleverest children seem always
the cruelest. At the sideshow we hear
them taunting a toddler too young
to understand, *You're a human being*
you're a human being as they ring
around the rosey. But have no fear,

dear ones. If the End dawns
luminous, only those who know
first-hand how monstrous being human
is, only genuine innocents will rise
unscathed above the leveled cities.
O very well then, such hyperbole.

If we can't abide how purely
children ape our unkindest cuts,
then let us teach them irony, tease
painful truth away and substitute
a simple fact: that word and act
forever play at odds, that heart
means not the harm we say and do.

Let the little bloomers frolic
at the Fair, where freaks will show
and tell their natural anomalies:
petrified man, century woman,
the dove-tailed, and the scaled not so
odd at all, quick to disarm a stare
and deftly undermine our fictions.

At the Folk Art Museum

Flood tide below me! I see you face to face!

Whitman never broke ranks
with the face vessels of the masses
we are and are ever unbecoming.
Shelved along a timeline they stare,
open-topped pots with broken teeth
and thin lips, lobed handles and balding
brims. Are their quirky reliefs filled
with visions of paradise or plots
against it? Usual stew of bad blood and
warm milk poured from head to head.

A man with a red beard and a deep voice.
A woman tinged with rosewater and soot,
muttering. Boy with a blue tongue, cool,
whose soup will go sour. Blond girl
under a torn veil, her sleeping eyes puffy.

After the hunt, the fire, and the end
of winter had been perfected, the mystery
the ancients savored most came
at the bottom of a crude mug. Not
sky nor beyond, not night and its
concealments, not rain nor wind, but
the human aspect fascinated, those
eyes and arched brows everywhere
inquiring, less other and ever stranger
for their likeness to our very own.

Aubade in Canis Major

Weaving down both sides of the road
we fancy ourselves uncommonly human,
tender as a god's living wounds. Blotto
on walkabout bleeding from the heels,
we squint at the Big Dog as if the dots
connected us, betting we were born
for higher things, forgetting the odds.

May the Great One heal us, feel for us,
pressing maze and seam into our skulls,
one plausible harmony. And so bemused
by the world, he gave a blessed sun to glint
off the broken glass. Reeling homeward
at dawn, we are the pains he took
to craft a sorry heaven of earth.

~~~~

4

Rapture Monday

Because we love them, the living dead
in their stylish graveclothes getting on the bus
or having lunch in the park, because
we love them, they do not look dead.

      Overhead, galaxies in deep space pinwheel
for eons into each other, diamond whirlpools
      hurling out blistering coronas and sidereal
travesties so far reaching even this noon
      sky would look like burning confetti—bang
and whimper—if we could close our eyes to see.

There is but one god after all—hand
at the throat, riptide so close to shore
we walk right into it and disappear, lovers,
believers for the rest of our lives.

Lightest Night of the Year

Earth is a dark star, the north
our season. A spruce has grown,
root and cone. Saw to the crux,
reverent, we bring it down.

Days pared inward, we take
the tree to the family room, raise
it rootless, hook angels
in the branches, string light.

Water it as if still alive
as if everything lasts on love
or liquid alone. Let it rise
toward a star far brighter.

Tie bundles by hand, set them
about for everyone to find. Sing.
Earth is a dark star bearing gifts,
giving rise to the dawn.

Gives rise to the spruce, gives rise
to the child who climbs it high
with a star in hand, a star
in mind, gives rise to the song.

The days grow brighter at both
ends. The tree lasts. New year,
it lies down to earth, burns,
glows, gives rise to the dark.

The Gift

The present arrives wrapped in silver,
in Mobius ribbons. 'Tis the season, each
facet of the box a mirror into which
we may gaze without seeing a future.
Tag names go *to* and *fro*, love evolving.
Inside knot and fold is a thing a human
hand crafted in a moment, all manner
of happy artifact, gizmo, figurine.

Open any present: flurry in a globe,
snow falling from wish to hand,
as if it could be held, ever, as if
the weather never changes. A gift
is given, forgiven, in time to let go,
now that the holy days are past.

Weather Vanes

If the prayer is well-made, wind
will stir the rain. Patience. A master
carver tools the oak, grain that flowed
for years, into fine intaglios: concavity
of rooster or butterfly, the fabulous
hoop-twirling bareback rider, or Lady
Liberty streamlined. Into the mold
the molten iron spills, dims and cools,
a perfect inverse of the wood,
the figure's charred valleys now hills.

Against this forged relief is hammered a sheet
of copper. Now a matching sheet.

Cut out, the twin halves are soldered
around a vertical rod, closed into a sleek
whole. When the hollow racehorse or
falling star ascends the barn, it swivels
freely on its axis, aerodynamic. North
wind sustains the chill it augurs,
the vane but one of many signifiers
that such creatures as rough hands
may craft of what is given, the more
to foresee the aims of providence.

End of August

Daylight cut back, bird chatter,
bug drone. The corn begins
to wither. Amazing, the casual approach
it takes. Riddles in a distant mind
grow common as weeds.

Afternoons, undercoats of cumulus
blue, darker than sky, and wind sweeps
up from the Gulf. In tight rows
that edge the plot, stalks browning,
late corn shuffles among friends.

Polite as elder strollers, arms
like weak flames, they bend ear-to-ear
asking *Did you hear?* or *Have you
any silk?* or *How are the lost?*
They wobble inside the breeze.

Scarecrow scatters his straw, shirt-
tail a flapping blackbird wing, his
pose too folksy to shoo the flock.
In his arms fewer cornflowers
open each dawn, cool dew flickering.

Inside the Buddha

Imagine the open mouths of museum
people. Flashlight and mirror, routine
check, they go electric upon finding
illustrated sutras in old Chinese.
Encached within the earthen idol
ancient scrolls will clarify the story
of the crafting of the Blessed One, how

a creed spread five thousand miles
from a single tree in India. The brittle
paper crackles true to its time, a fine
dust rising, each inked character
bold as any one of ten thousand acts,
compassionate or crusading. Already
translated are dates and one village

heretofore unknown: Chinmancun,
1155. Scholars will come to know
that world in light of every extant
text, though anyone can guess
the renunciant who hid these here
feared the Emperor, hoped the army
would not search behind a placid gaze

set in stone. The figure, the *bodhisattva*,
sits poised with loving concern
for others, even retrospective future
generations, their smooth young faces
rapt, who reach white-gloved inside
the statue's hollow to deliver these
illuminations into artificial light.

The Architecture of Sunlight

Imagine the sandstone sun just
before down, streaming through
the lattice of the garret's
broad windows: dusk orange
levered up on the far wall.
Even your room inclines westward,
somber shadows to begin.

As the ceiling admits to evening,
a skylight slopes in the kitchen.
Open it slowly, a single pane leveling
reflection. Along the hip rafter's
diagonal, a tapestry arcs into the wedge
of a spare room. Day's heat rises
from downstairs and peaks

and goes out. Later, the candles.
The way you gaze toward
the sky beyond the glass is no
fiction. Where all beams
converge is the center of your
thought, a minor chord scissored,
gimlet sun refurling inward.

The Stairs from Above

Velvet sleeves the railing. The tatter
registers gray among blacker
and whiter tones. Iron balusters
climb toward you. Gallery stairway
curves upward, lifting highlights
from the main floor in a lazy,
serrated vortex. Step down them

into the pretty picture of:
blustery afternoon, four friends
and I (and the Saturday man)
found more refuge than art.
The floor a checkerboard, the stairs
from above like the arc of a wheel
with lucky numbers. I'm telling you

because the camera unsteadies.
By simple tokens, chance moves
the cavalry against windmills. In turn,
the moment wobbles in the lens
which blurs the picture. You,
as you look around, look up.
Catch the photographer

leaning over the rail guessing
depth of field. See him, you've
seen the proof: from the square
roots of abyss, upward through
every seeing eye, pass
what memory plays, what
captured pieces.

Day of Rest

Hustling from morning sacraments
to the afternoon game, people stop,
homeward, to shop for everything
they need: live batteries and bottled
water, two-for-one. The aisles brim
with browsers combing blue-light bins
to crown a week of work well done,
another one begun.

It takes an hour to find a belt that fits.
A boy says to his father *Let's just stop*
in toys before we go. Back home
I exercise my other options.
Saturday's wantonness past, Monday's
ghostly face afloat, the rooftop
aerials vibrate sympathetically
with church bell medleys.

For handsome pay, an American hero
rolls his ankle on artificial turf,
holds the game ball on the sidelines.
On bended knees, I stretch my head
back and breathe the blue, devoted
air. A whistle blows play dead.
Digits on the scoreboard clock
stop counting down to the news.

Half-Lives

Unlike the brief neutrino a brittle maple
leaf will fall for months without landing.
Bare branchwork wires the twilight
passing through it—double exposure—
into my eye. The radioactive elements
decay into decimals geometrically
but never to nothing: half since
the Great War, half by a blue moon,
half at New Year's, half
this week, half
again.

What remains are microscopic
phosphors, barely enough light
for vacant lots in the hour of trances:
the city a shuttered eye, photon trail
across the film, skeleton silhouette.
Heart quickens when a slick

leaf undercuts my step. In a darkroom
tray, flash develops into knifeblade.
In the background of the scene,

a fire escape. A figure drifts up
elapsing into broken glass.

Litany

Lost continents of no doubt higher cultures,
the famous lost tribes, whole years lost in search of.
Lost acuities, lost causes, lost glaciers,
lost dogs, and moreover, dog tags fallen
in muddy impressions of combat boot-soles,
how all washed away. And how paradise was lost:
bad angel wanted his halo back, too badly.

All the lost children of conflict, neglect,
cruelty, and shame. Never forgive yourself.
Lost in action, lost in thought, listing
every name and losing count, left to grinding
driftwood sticks together, furious for light
that's lost inside them, for a loser weeps but not
in words, and then is lost without them.

Intermedial

Trouble kill my brother
Got me one foot in my grave.

BIG BILL BROONZY

It's not the end. It's just beginning
to end. Though the Great Decline
fell before the Middle Ages, anyone
at fifty might see the world as a dog
turned suddenly vicious. A betting
man begins by backing off. It's not
his dog. But if youth has hedged well
against age, he might still kill
for a love that makes him whole.

In Byzantium, he could have done so—
killers were forgiven. But let him be
caught cutting cloth of royal purple
or teaching the enemy shipbuilding,
and he could be drowned in a brown sack
with a cock and a viper. In latter days
the Byzantines came to favor mutilation:
a tongueless wretch might take a lifetime
to repent high treason and never tell.

So death hounds the middle years,
seldom promising martyrdom.
A crow can live to a hundred—let it—
there's plenty of carrion. But if
a man wants to quit this minute,
as fifty more acres of rainforest topple
to profit, let him count the broken
bones that line the shadow of Mt. Fuji,
that most scenic of lovers' leaps.

From zygote quarks to grandmother
stars, the body blooms and wilts, fond
of transitory states. Much that dissolves
in passing, one more hour of living
essentially restores. The pains a graying
guitarist feels in his thumbs he kneads
into walking blues. The verses might
keep coming, indefinitely high or low,
sung to no end, a song to make it so.

"Kings of Boogie"

after Savoy Brown

The stage rises through floodwall shadow.
One monster Frisbee-toss down the bank
the swelled Ohio muddles into spring.
Thin crowd. The barefoot singer jokes
the band's true fans must be in jail,
motorcycles parked at bars, forgotten.

It's never enough he announces: I'm
guessing booze, sex, cash, applause.
If we dig the hits, he can buy some shoes.
Sun in cool decline, up-loud blues
reverb off downtown bricks and off
the far-side river bluffs another second
later. It's almost enough for me. Then

the singer tells the cops to get fucked.
Just kidding, officer he elucidates, crowd
stirring as the crew breaks down
makeshift gates. Sudden encore underway,
we straggling rockers clap in time,
choice last words wailed upstream.

The elderly approach, their little dogs
and Sunday walks askance, and fading
waves of bass ripple the polyester a little.
Like the teens, they don't know the band,
only that the beat's gone off. Not one
to let go of the past too delicately,
if ever, I keep shouting requests.

The Evolution of Rock 'n Roll

When Elvis left the federal building
he was humming in Seconal haze,
casting glittered shadows on the flag.

Now the Graceland bathroom is a maze
of aging boomers, the company offices
automated, the concert stages on fire.

The King's megawatt tower—WXYR—
toppled for a dealership, fat Hummers
line the lot, gleaming for all creation
like Brinks trucks, a choice of six colors.

Each one sold can blast a load of classics,
three hundred watts and two sub-woofers,
so far off-road that nothing echoes
in the suburbs but credit card jingles,
elevator filler, and a suicide rag.

Monday Underworld

Up Saturday night's mad
mountain we clambered, piano solo
drifting, fits of brilliance.

Muted bash of cymbals
harrowed ears, and dancing finally
scored the rime on our eyes.

Sunday morning we rested, cathedral
sunlight stained glass haloes.
Noon, we cast the first loaded die,

week of new woe. Snake eye.
The tower clock is grinding
gears, rusted rewind. Monday sirens

call us back, destiny manifest.
Once more steeply down and out
of the singing we step.

Tantamount

Clicks and sorry squawks rattle the oak
outside. First warm day of spring
and even birds with no gift try warbling.
That's why I'm writing you. It snowed
here yesterday, chilly incongruity.
Against the bard's appeal, we'd
best admit impediment. Want to know

why? That's why. Years playing *Go*,
plonking stones on a dumb grid,
we walled each other off, comings
and leavings. The artist formerly known
as *darling*, I'm worn down to sour notes.
Hell's thawed. We should know how
to play the game alone by now.

Interlude

On the sidewalk some girls
have discovered glare ice
         spared
from the March thaw by
shadow.
Out my north window: sudden
shrieks unhemmed.
            Nevermind
earrings and permanents, they
do not pass up the chance to
run and slide
         quick turn
     to see how far.
Looking backward
         with a pleasure
that briefly repeals
the laws of motion, they take
        a full measure.

Wish Well

Musing aloud, the veiled genie and
the gifted fish agree your wants are ill-
conceived, too tricky to spell out.
In mind so simple, pennies in a font,
but in the enchanted forest where
every wish is said and done—behold—
the granting warps them inside out.

World peace, so nobly implored,
unfolds as endless fields of graves,
no one left but you and blackbirds
chittering in charred wind. Next,
your fame or fortune, hastily ordered,
comes overcooked, a shiny wheelchair
on the side. And granted, the fabled

King who spent his human touch
learned the hard way how gold is
foiled in the getting and love—imagine!—
is gotten in the giving. And by some
magic unequivocal, one last wish
may well and wisely undo all the rest,
and you yourself come true.

Photograph © Sandee Lloyd

A. E. STRINGER is the author of two collections of poems, *Channel Markers* (Wesleyan University Press) and *Human Costume* (Salmon Poetry). His work has appeared in such journals as *The Nation*, *Antaeus*, *The Ohio Review*, *Denver Quarterly*, *Prairie Schooner*, *Shenandoah*, *Poetry Northwest*, and in *Backcountry: Contemporary Writing in West Virginia*. He also edited and introduced an edition of Louise McNeill's *Paradox Hill* (West Virginia University Press). For twenty-four years, he has taught writing and literature at Marshall University.

ALSO BY A. E. STRINGER

Channel Markers

Human Costume

Paradox Hill: From Appalachia to Lunar Shore
by Louise McNeill
Edited with an introduction by A. E. Stringer